MW00914846

# 1,000 Interesting Facts

## Fun Facts to Kill Some Time and Have Fun with Your Family

**Adam Anderson**

PUBLISHED BY:

Adam Anderson

Copyright © 2012

# Table of Contents

# The Human Body

1) There are one trillion germs that live on each human foot
2) A man's heartbeat is slower than a woman's heartbeat
3) When a person is frightened, their ears produce more earwax
4) If your spit can't dissolve whatever food you're eating, you can't taste it
5) It takes seven seconds for the food you ingested to go from your mouth to your stomach
6) Your nose is the same size as your thumb
7) As every finger print is different so is your tongue print
8) Eight percent of the body's weight is in your blood
9) Every 3-5 months, your eyebrow hair sheds
10) Your eyelashes can last up to 150 days

## Domestic Cats

1) There are 100 different vocal sounds a cat can make, whereas a dog can only make 10

2) A cat's whisker length can help you determine what they can fit into
3) Cats can sleep up to 16 hours a day
4) There are 32 muscles in a cat's ear
5) Cats can run up to 31 miles an hour
6) A cat's nose-print is unique to a cat just like fingerprints in humans
7) Egyptians worshiped cats in ancient times
8) Cats can jump up to six feet in the air
9) A cat will spend about 11,000 hours of its life purring
10) Sideways jaw movements are impossible for a cat

## Hamsters

1) Like a pig, a female hamster is called a sow, and a male hamster is called a boar
2) Hamsters are colorblind
3) Food they've gathered in the wild are stored in the expandable pouches in their cheeks which they later distribute to their colony
4) Cedar products cause an allergic reaction in most hamsters
5) If the hamster's head can fit through a crack, the rest of its body can
6) They can only see six inches in front of them

7) Hamsters can reach up to 200 pounds in weight
8) Hamsters puff up their checks with air in order to swim
9) Hamsters became pets in the 1930s
10) In the wild, some hamsters can become the size of guinea pigs

# Fish

1) Fish have been on the earth for over 450 million years
2) The Spotted Climbing Perch can walk on land for short distances
3) Goldfish don't have eyelids
4) Fish range from a third of an inch in size to 50 feet
5) Goldfish have been pets for over 1,000 years
6) Fish scales are used in some lipsticks
7) There are more fish than mammals, birds, reptiles, and amphibians all put together
8) Fish were around before the dinosaurs
9) Some fish make sounds by grinding their teeth and also rattling their bones
10) Forty percent of the different species of fish are found in fresh water

# Butterflies and Caterpillars

1) Despite having 12 eyes, the caterpillars do not have excellent eyesight
2) Some caterpillars can grow up to 12 inches long
3) Butterflies fly 12 miles an hour
4) Antarctica is the only place you can't find a butterfly
5) Butterflies do not feed only from flowers but also on rotting fruits and dung
6) Male Swallowtail butterflies will gather at puddles to drink the mud
7) Monarch butterflies are poisonous to birds, so they won't eat them
8) Caterpillars don't have bones but use 1,000 muscles to move
9) Butterflies can lay up to 500 eggs
10) Butterflies' antennae are used to smell things

# Comics

1) If you wanted to buy the first Superman comic, it's going to cost you $150,000
2) In Japan, more paper are used to make comics than to make toilet paper

3) The cartoon poster for the Disney movie "Alice's Day at the Sea" sold $36,534 at a London auction in 1994
4) "Keep 'em flying" was a slogan in WW2; this was also Wonder Woman's battle cry
5) The Hulk originally was grey and not green
6) When comics first came out, they were only 10 cents
7) *Calvin and Hobbes*, created by Bill Waterson, first came out in 1985
8) *The Far Side*, by Gary Larson, sold over six million copies by 1987
9) Jim Davis's *Garfield* is in seven different languages and printed in 22 different countries
10) On July 20, 2006, the United States Postal Service issued stamps that featured superheroes

## Knights

1) Young men training to be knights would ride piggyback to work on their balance
2) When jousting, knights would carry a Lady's "favour"; this is her scarf or handkerchief
3) It took 14 years of training to become a knight

4) Coup de Grace is the name of a death blow a knight would give to his mortally wounded opponent
5) At the end of knighthood, they were given the title, "Sir"
6) As part of his services, the knight would get land, and this was called a "fief"
7) Knights began their training at seven years old
8) The suit of armor worn by a knight weighed about 50 pounds
9) It's rare for non-nobility to gain knighthood through battle
10) Knighthood still exists today as a term of honor

## Swords

1) Medieval swords weighed around 6-10 pounds
2) Medieval swords were commonly made from steel
3) The broadsword is the earliest medieval sword and originated from the 6th century
4) A medieval broadsword was used to cut and slice an opponent
5) Keeping a sword in a leather casing too long can cause it to rust

6) Egyptians used their swords only for life or death circumstances
7) Rapiers became open to the public in the 16th century for fencing
8) Samurai swords were tested out on prisoners
9) Ancient Greeks made their swords from bronze and copper
10) Chalos was a copper sword used by Greek foot soldiers

## Money

1) Forty-three pounds and 7 1/4 ounce is the heaviest coin recorded; it's from Sweden
2) In the past, cows, salt, jewels, and shark's teeth were used as money
3) The largest check ever written was for $1,279,187,490
4) If someone stacked $1 million in $1 bills, it would reach 361 feet high
5) It costs 4.2 cents to make a bill in the U.S.
6) Twenty-six million money notes are made a day
7) Forty-five percent of money made is in the form of $1 bills/coins

8) In 1916, you could bring your money to the bank to be washed, ironed, and given back to you
9) The first paper money was made in China
10) Since 1969, the $100 bill is the largest bill you can get

## Samurai

1) A samurai is a warrior in service to their lord (or Daimyo)
2) Bushido, or the way of the warrior, is the code of the samurai that consisted of honor, loyalty, and mastery of martial arts until death
3) Seppuku is a ritual suicide that a samurai followed, which meant they would rather die by their own sword than be held captive by their enemies
4) Katana is the samurai's sword, which is his primary weapon
5) Yumi is a long bow; Kyujutsu means skill of the bow, which is the mastery of the Yumi
6) Ronin is a Samurai without a Daimyo
7) Their armor weighs 60 pounds
8) Wakizashi is the samurai's short blade
9) A Tessen fan is made from metal; this weapon comes in handy in places

where swords or other overt weapons
are not allowed

10) Samurai women wore sharp hairpins in
their hair as a backup weapon

# Ninja

1) Ninja, in the Kunyomi language, is
Shinobi, which means "steal away"
2) Ninjas were so secretive that little is
known about them
3) The highest rank to the lowest rank of
a Shinobi is Jonin, Chunin, and Genin
4) Ninjas were mostly hired by Daimyos
5) They generally disguised themselves
as priests, fortunetellers, merchants,
and monks
6) Some of their weapons were battle
fans, kunai, kyoketsu-shogue (long
spears), and shurikens
7) Folklore described them as half-man
and half-crow
8) Ninjutsu is the art of stealth
9) Yamabushi, also called monk warriors,
were among the first ninja
10) Samurai lords would hire them to do
their dirty work

# Cows

1) Cows have 32 teeth
2) They can live to be 25 years old
3) Cows can climb stairs but cannot go down them
4) Cows can weigh about 1,400 pounds
5) They produce up to 10 tons of manure a year
6) Cows can make up to 125 pounds of saliva a day
7) Cows stand up and sit down about 14 times a day
8) Thirty pounds of urine is what the average cow produces in a day
9) Cows make around 40,000 jaw movements a day
10) Cows produce 200,000 glasses of milk in one lifetime

# Coca-Cola

1) Coca-Cola has been a favorite drink for over 100 years
2) Coca-Cola was created in May 1886
3) Over 1 billion cans are consumed each day

4) At one time, the company could barely sell eight glasses a day
5) Santa Claus (as we know him now) with his red suit and white beard was conceptualized and created for a Coca Cola ad
6) Coca-Cola was invented in Atlanta, GA by Doctor John Pemberton
7) The company has over 70 different flavors of Fanta Soda, one of its soft drinks, around the world
8) Coca-Cola was first made to be a medicine
9) Coca-Cola can be found in 200 different countries
10) Coca-Cola first operated in Canada in 1904

## Rabbits

1) A rabbit's teeth never stop growing
2) Rabbits can be trained to use a litter box
3) Rabbits cannot vomit
4) A group of rabbits is called a herd
5) A four-pound rabbit can drink as much as a 20-pound dog
6) Rabbits do not hibernate
7) Domestic rabbits can't mate with wild ones

8) Rabbits can only sweat on the pads of their feet
9) Rabbits can jump up to 36 inches when they are scared
10) Rabbits have 28 teeth

# Pants

1) Ankle-length pants have been worn by workers since 1788
2) Pants represented equality amongst the French people
3) Inuit pants have two layers to keep heat close to the body
4) Before the 19th century, pants were referred to as underwear in the United Kingdom
5) Other words for pants are breeches, slacks, kex, and strides
6) Levi's jeans were first invented in 1891
7) Two hundred and fifteen jeans can be made from one bale of cotton
8) In North America, the average person owns seven pairs of pants
9) July 27 is Take Your Pants for a Walk Day
10) Donald Duck cartoons were banned in Finland because he doesn't wear any pants

# Cars

1) The first car was made in 1769
2) By 1950, the United States had over 50 million cars
3) Chevrolet Impala broke the record for sales in 1961
4) The first cars used levers instead of wheels
5) Ferrari makes up to 30 cars a day
6) 14 milliseconds is how long it takes an airbag to go off
7) Tata made the world's cheapest car, the Tata Nano
8) Women introduced the windshield wiper
9) Siegfried Marcus built the first car engine
10) Benz was the first car offered for sale

## Nail Polish

1) A clear nail polish can fix chips in car windows
2) Wearing clear nail polish makes your nails less prone to breaking
3) French royalty had everyone in their court get their nails done, hence, the name French Manicure

4) In the 1950s, wearing bright nail polish made you a "bad" girl, and you couldn't wear it to church
5) The most expensive bottle to date is worth $250,000
6) Unopened nail polish can last two years
7) Nail polish remover never expires
8) It was once used to identify leaf fossils
9) These metals give nail polish its shine: aluminum, copper, gold, and zinc
10) Frequent use of nail polish stain your nails

## Watches

1) The first wristwatches had to be wound by hand to work
2) Actual rubies were used to keep a watch running; now fake rubies are used
3) Rolex invented the first waterproof watch
4) Rolex is the most popular counterfeit watch in the world
5) Before watches and clocks, people used sundials and hourglasses

6) Wrist watches with alarms were first made by watch manufacturer Eterna in 1908
7) The first watch was designed before the 16th century in Italy
8) Watch parts were made by hand until 1850
9) Apollo program astronauts wore Omega wrist watches
10) The very first watches were very heavy and decorated with crosses, bones, and flowers

## Manga

1) In Japanese, it means whimsical pictures
2) Like Japanese literature, it is read right to left
3) Unlike comics in Canada and the United States, Manga is present in part color
4) Manga has been around since the 19th century
5) All Manga is drawn by hand
6) Tezuka Osamu is the most popular Manga artist in Japan
7) The first Manga was made by Choujuugiga

8) Calling it Manga was the idea of Rakuten Kitazawa
9) In 2008, Canadians and Americans bought over $175 million of Manga
10) Manga targeted for women readers is called shojo

## Kangaroos

1) A male kangaroo is called a boomer; a female is a flyer
2) Kangaroo means, "I don't understand," in the Australian native language
3) There are 40 different types of kangaroos
4) The smallest kangaroo is called a wallaby
5) The largest kangaroo is the red kangaroo
6) The largest kangaroo weighs 300 pounds
7) Kangaroos can hop at 40 miles per hour
8) Kangaroos can go months without drinking
9) Most kangaroos can only move their hind legs together and not one at a time
10) Kangaroos live in groups called mobs

# Badger

1) There are 7 different species of badgers worldwide
2) Badgers can eat rattlesnakes
3) The ferret badger will sleep in trees
4) Badgers belong to the weasel family
5) The badger's name comes from the French word, "becheur," which means digger
6) The badger's life span is 14 years
7) Badgers live in groups called clans
8) Male badgers are called boars, and females are called sows
9) Badgers can become intoxicated after eating rotten fruits
10) Badgers can usually be found in open prairies and plains

# Halloween

1) The first Jack O'Lantern was made from turnips
2) Samhainophobia is the fear of Halloween
3) Halloween is short for All Hallow's Eve, or Hallow's Evening

4) Ireland is believed to be the birthplace of Halloween
5) It was believed that if you wear your clothes inside-out and walk backwards all day, you'll see a witch at midnight
6) Halloween has been around for over 6,000 years and is thought to have originated in 4000 B.C.
7) 110 million doors will be knocked on Halloween night
8) In the U.S., candy sales are around $2 million just for Halloween
9) The movie *Halloween* was made in 21 days and had almost no budget
10) On the Halloween of 1926, the famous magician Harry Houdini died

# Bats

1) There are 1,240 different bats in the world
2) Fox bats are also called mega-bats
3) Most bats live in groups called colonies
4) The smallest bat weighs as much as a dime
5) Each bat can eat between 2,000 to 6,000 bugs each night
6) Vampire bats drink a tablespoon of blood per night and from animals only

7) Vampire bats are very social and will feed the elderly and sick bats when they need it
8) Some bats have twins
9) Blood doesn't rush to their heads because they are too small for gravity to affect them
10) Less than 1% of bats have rabies

## Cameras

1) There are three types of video cameras: consumer, prosumer, and professional
2) The oldest picture known with a man on it was taken in Paris. The picture shows a gentleman having his shoes shine
3) The camera is basically a lightproof box with a hole in it
4) The first photograph was done by Joseph Draper
5) In 1900, Kodak sells camera for $1 and a film for 15 cents
6) The first digital camera cost $10,000
7) 2.5 billion people around the world have digital cameras
8) The first underwater photo was taken in 1856

9) The first colored photograph was created in 1861
10) In 2003, digital cameras beat film cameras in sales worldwide

## Video Games

1) In 1947, the first interactive game was made
2) In 1955, the first computer you could play chess with was built
3) The first coin-operated game cost 10 cents for one game and 25 cents for three
4) Pac-Man was at its most popular in the 1980s
5) Sega came out in 1983
6) Matt Damon do not want to appear in the game Bourne Conspiracy because he thinks it is too violent
7) Mario (*Super Mario*) was the name of the creator's landlord
8) A man who is addicted to playing PlayStation 2 changed his last name legally to PlayStation 2.
9) Mario (*Super Mario*) has appeared in 120 video games
10) Atari is named after the Japanese word for success

# Board Games

1) The game Yathzee was made by a Canadian couple who loves to entertain their guests on their yacht with the game
2) There are 54 wooden blocks in the game Jenga
3) In Hungry Hungry Hippos, the purple hippo's name is Lizzie, the green one is Homer, the red one is Henry and the yellow hippo is Harry while their surnames are all Hippo
4) Sorry was invented in 1929
5) Monopoly was played for ten days inside an elevator
6) Murder was a board game created as a pastime during the air raids of World War II and then later on the game was re-named as what we know now as the game Clue
7) Chess is the most popular board game in the world and Monopoly is the second most popular board game
8) No one knows why there are jokers in a deck of cards
9) Snakes and Ladders originated from India's 16th century Chutes and Ladder
10) There are 1240 versions of Monopoly

# Anime

1) Anime is the Japanese style of animation
2) Astro Boy was one of the first anime to gain popularity
3) The first anime was done in 1917
4) In the 1980s, anime started getting popular outside of Japan
5) Clamp is an anime/manga group that is made up of an all female staff
6) Felix the Cat is one of the earliest anime translated in the U.S.
7) Miyazaki Films, one of the top anime feature filmmakers, started in the 1980s
8) Studio Ghibli films are amazingly popular worldwide; Studio Ghibli made eight out of the 15 highest grossing anime films
9) All anime is first hand drawn
10) About 160,000 people a month look up the anime Dragon Ball Z on the internet

# Dogs

1) Ozzy Osborne saved his wife's dog by tackling a coyote that was attacking it

2) Dogs have sweat glands on their paw pads
3) The shoulder blades of a dog remain unattached to allow more movement for running
4) The most dogs ever owned by one person was 5,000
5) The most popular names for dogs are Max, Jake, Molly, and Maggie
6) Dachshunds were bred to hunt badgers
7) Dalmatians are completely white at birth
8) Puppies are born blind, deaf, and toothless
9) Basenji dogs cannot bark
10) It takes $10,000 to train and certify a search-and-rescue dog

## Valentine's Day

1) One billion Valentine's Day cards are given in North America alone on this day
2) Women buy 85% of cards for Valentines worldwide
3) Fifty million roses are bought worldwide each year for Valentine's Day

4) Seventy-three percent of men buy flowers for Valentines
5) Rome celebrated this day in honor of Juno, the goddess of women and marriage
6) In medieval times, girls ate strange things in order to dream of their future husband
7) In 1537, it was officially declared a holiday in England by King Henry VIII
8) Thirty-five million heart-shaped boxes are sold each year
9) Fifteen percent of women send themselves flowers on Valentine's Day
10) Teachers receive the most Valentine's Day cards, followed by children, mothers, and pets

## Flowers

1) Roses are related to apples and pears
2) In the 1600s, tulips were more valuable than gold in Holland
3) In a recipe that calls for onions, you can use a tulip bulb as a substitute
4) Saffron comes from the flower, Crocus
5) The oldest flower bloomed 125 million years ago in China; it looked like a lily
6) Sunflowers move with the sun
7) Moon flowers bloom at night only

8) Yarrow, when drank as a tea, was once believed to cure influenza and heal the wounds of World War I soldiers
9) The lotus is considered to be sacred by the ancient Egyptians and is used for burial rituals
10) Angelica were used for almost every ailment and to ward off evil spirits by the Native Americans

## Trees

1) Trees are the longest living organisms on land
2) Trees cut down noise pollution
3) The world's oldest living tree, the Methuselah, is 4,600 years old
4) The tallest tree is 379 feet tall
5) People would literally die without trees to convert carbon dioxide to oxygen
6) Trees lower air temperature
7) A tree makes 260 pounds of oxygen a year
8) Trees make water cleaner by filtering rain
9) Trees protect us from rain, hail, snow, and ice
10) Trees can cool a building by 20 percent.

# Geodes

1) Geodes is from the Latin meaning "earthlike"
2) They range from 1-30 inches in size
3) Quartz is the dominant form of geodes
4) Their origins still puzzle people to this date
5) It can take hundreds of millions of years to create the inside of a geode
6) They come in variety of different colors
7) Rare ones can be worth thousands of dollars
8) You can't tell what kind they are until you open them
9) They are formed in the bubbles of volcanic rocks
10) They are commonly in two forms: crystals or solid

# Bears

1) Bears are part of the Ursidae family
2) A male is called a boar or he-bear, and the female is called a sow or she-bear
3) They can weigh up to 1,000 pounds
4) Bears hibernate 3-5 months

5) Bears are related to pandas, dogs, and raccoons
6) Some types of bears are considered endangered
7) When hibernating, a bear's heartbeats go down to eight beats a minute
8) Ninety-eight percent of grizzlies live in Alaska
9) Polar bears can swim 100 miles without rest
10) The koala bear's name comes from their aboriginal name which means, "animal that does not drink"

## Shoes

1) Shoe fashion started in 1663
2) In the 9th and 10th centuries, the highest royalty wore wooden shoes
3) In 1927, X-rays were used to help with shoe fitting
4) The first women's boot was designed for Queen Victoria
5) In Biblical times, sandals were given as a sign of an oath
6) In Hungary, the groom makes a toast out of the bride's shoe
7) Sneakers were originally called keds
8) Heels in the 16th and 17th centuries were always red in color

9) Heels were invented in the Middle East to get feet off burning sand
10) Shoes were made over 4,000 years ago

# Glass

1) Stone Age men used naturally formed glass as a weapon and as a tool
2) Glass takes over one million years to decompose
3) The energy saved from one recycled bottle can run a 100-watt light bulb for four hours
4) Recycling glass reduced air pollution by 20% and water pollution by 50%
5) Cracks in glass move at 3,000 miles per hour
6) In the 1800s, window glass became high in demand
7) In 1960s, the first bottle collecting plants were made
8) Stained glass is regular glass with color added
9) Ancient Egyptians and Romans used stain glass as cups and bowls
10) The first glass containers were made by Ancient Egyptians in 1500 BC

# Books

1) Some books that were rejected multiple times but are now famous are J.K Rowling's *Harry Potter and the Philosopher's Stone* and Beatrice Potter's *The Tale of Peter Rabbit*

2) Two books written while in prison were *De Profundis* by Oscar Wilde and *The Prince* by Machiavelli

3) Euclid's *Elements* is the most successful textbook in history. It has over 1,000 editions

4) The first published recipe book was done in 1390 A.D.

5) Literature didn't appear until the 9th century

6) Paper was invented in China in 105 A.D.

7) Cinderella first appeared in a book in the 850s in China

8) The first novel was written by a Japanese noblewoman; it was entitled *The Tale of Genji*

9) Shakespeare used 29,000 different words; 10,000 of them were not found in surviving literature before

10) Edgar Allen Poe wrote a story in 1838 about a shipwreck and how three survivors killed and ate a man, Richard Parker; in 1884, in real life,
this actually happened to a man called Richard Parker.

## Christmas

1) Scientists calculated that Santa Claus would have to visit 822 homes a second on Christmas Eve in order to visit everyone in one night
2) In the short form of Christmas, X-mas, the "X" is the Greek short form of Christ
3) There is a town in Indiana called Santa Claus
4) Electric lights were first used on trees in 1895
5) The first Christmas stamp was issued in 1943 in Austria
6) The first card was designed by J.C. Horsley in 1843
7) The poinsettia in Mexico, its native location, is referred to as "The Flower of the Holy Night"
8) Mistletoe was associated with peace and friendship

9) Three billion Christmas cards are sold in the U.S. alone
10) Christmas sales represent one-sixth of U.S. retail sales

## Mushrooms

1) Mushrooms can both cure and cause diseases
2) An expert about mushrooms is called a mycologist
3) Truffles have been collected for over 3,600 years
4) Truffles can cost $400 an ounce
5) Puffball spores were used by Native Americans to help slow bleeding
6) Mushroom circles will die if they contact another mushroom circle
7) Mushrooms rings can grow as large as 30 feet wide
8) Mushrooms are virtually sodium and fat free
9) There are about two million types of mushrooms in the world
10) The Portabella mushroom contained more potassium than banana

# Easter goodies

1) Over 90 million Easter bunnies are made each year worldwide
2) Sixteen billion jelly beans are made for Easter each year
3) The largest jar of jelly beans was 6,050 pounds
4) Seventy-five percent of kids will do extra chores for more Easter candy
5) The first chocolate eggs were made in Europe
6) Forty-two percent of people prefer the solid chocolate rabbit, followed by the hollow bunnies and the marshmallow filled bunnies, over other candies for Easter
7) Seventy-six percent of people eat the ears of a chocolate rabbit first
8) Milk chocolate is preferred by 65% of adults
9) At one time, pretzels were given out at Easter, as well as chocolate
10) In the olden times, hot cross buns were given out as Easter treats by monks

# Chocolate

1) Two thousand years ago, Mayan Indians grounded cocoa beans for drinking
2) Mayan Indians used cocoa beans as money
3) In the 1700s, chocolate houses were more popular than coffee houses
4) Chocolate comes from the Aztec word xocolatl, meaning "bitter water"
5) Chocolate is a natural antidepressant
6) Chocolate is poisonous to dogs and other small animals
7) Chocolate makers use 40% of the world's almonds
8) Chocolate first appeared in the solid form in the 18th century
9) In 1875, milk chocolate was created
10) In 1907, the Hershey Kiss factory started making 33 million Kisses per day

# Friday the 13th

1) In France, if you're uncomfortable with 13 guests, you can hire a 14th one
2) A university in Delaware has studied Friday the 13th for over 20 years

3) A fear of it is called paraskavedekatriaphbia
4) Butch Cassidy was born on a Friday the 13th
5) No one knows the origins of this fear
6) Italians feel the same about Friday the 17th as most do about Friday the 13th
7) Henry Ford refused to do business on Friday the 13th
8) The British Navy built a ship called Friday the 13th, and when it left dock, it was never heard from again
9) Hospitals don't have 13th floor or a Room 13
10) Friday the 13th happens at least once a year and up to three times a year

## Monday

1) Originally, Monday got its name from the moon
2) Fifty percent of employees are late on a Monday
3) The French call their lemon-colored cars "Monday cars"
4) Car salesmen are most likely to cut a deal on a Monday
5) If you were born on a Monday, it is said you will be fair of face

6) People who suffer from the Monday syndrome are between 45-54 years of age
7) The most common day to have a heart attack is on a Monday
8) Garfield (the cat) hates Mondays
9) There are either 52 or 53 Mondays every year
10) "Blue Monday" is when blue-collar workers begin their work week

## Rats

1) Ancient Romans considered rats lucky
2) Rats can swim and generally enjoy it
3) Rats starred or appeared in over 400 films
4) Rats are colorblind
5) A group of rats is called a mischief
6) Rats live 2-6 years
7) Rats are the first animal in the Chinese Zodiac
8) The teeth of rats never stop growing
9) Rats use their tails for balance and to regulate their temperature
10) More than 20,000 rats live in a Hindu temple in India in honor of the rat goddess Kata Mata

# Hummingbird

1) There are over 330 types of hummingbirds
2) Hummingbirds are the world's smallest bird
3) Hummingbirds can fly up, down, sideways, and upside down
4) Hummingbirds average 50 flaps per second
5) Hummingbirds live on the average for four years
6) Hummingbirds can't walk or hop
7) Hummingbirds have 1,000-1,500 feathers
8) At rest, hummingbirds take an average of 250 breaths per second
9) Hummingbirds eat every 10 minutes because they have high metabolism
10) Hummingbirds can fly up to 60 miles per hour

# Penguin

1) There are 18 types of penguins in the world

2) Most penguins are found in the southern, not in the northern part of the world
3) Penguins cannot fly but are fast swimmers
4) The classic coloring of penguins supplies them with protection in water
5) Penguins see better in the water than out of it
6) The largest penguin can weigh up to 90 pounds
7) King penguins don't make nests but take turns holding their eggs in their feet
8) Penguins can live 15-20 years
9) Penguins spend 75% of their lives in water
10) Penguins can reach heights of up to 40 inches tall

## Elephants

1) Elephants have poor eyesight
2) The African elephant and the Asian elephant are the two types of elephants in the world
3) The ears of an elephant are used to keep them cool

4) An adult elephant can reach 10-13 feet in height
5) Adult elephants can weigh up to 11,000 pounds
6) Elephants can live up to 70 years
7) Elephants eat 500 pounds of food each day
8) Elephants have the largest brain among the land animals
9) They are the only mammals that can't jump
10) Elephants use their trunks to breathe underwater and swim for long distances

# Mice

1) The name mouse comes from the Sanskrit word "mus," which means thief
2) Mice can make their own vitamin C
3) The mouse body is as long as its tail
4) A baby mouse is called a kitten
5) At one time, people thought fried mouse or mouse pie stopped bedwetting
6) Mickey Mouse was created in 1928
7) The Japanese bred the white mouse over 300 years ago

8) Wild mice only live for about five months
9) Mice can breed up to 10 times a year
10) Mice eat 10-20 times a day

# Computer

1) The first programmable computer was created in 1936
2) In the 1940s, computers were so huge that they took up whole rooms
3) The internet began in 1969
4) There are 6,000 new computer viruses each month
5) Doug Englebart created the first computer mouse
6) Stewardesses is the longest word that can be typed with the left-hand side of the keyboard
7) Tetris has sold over 100 million copies
8) Twelve people designed the IBM PC; they were known as the "Dirty Dozen"
9) A bit is the smallest piece of computer information
10) It was estimated that by 2012, 17 billion computers connected to the internet

# Platypus

1) The platypus can only be found in Eastern Australia
2) The platypus has pouches inside its cheeks that it used to store food temporarily
3) The platypus is one of the five mammals that lay eggs
4) The platypus hunts and mates underwater but lives on land
5) The platypus weighs around six pounds
6) The platypus lives up to 12 years
7) Females can have up to three eggs at one time
8) The platypus is carnivorous
9) The platypus swims with its eyes, ears, and nose shut
10) The platypus spends 12 hours each day searching for food

# Hair

1) Hair is considered the second fastest growing tissue in the body, next to bone marrow
2) Red hair is the rarest hair color

3) Greeks believed that redheads would turn into vampires when they died
4) Blonde hair grows faster than brown hair
5) Warm weather promotes hair growth so your hair grows faster in the summer
6) On average, an individual has 100,000 hairs
7) Redheads have the thickest hair
8) People lose more hair when they are on a crash diet
9) Hair color gets determined in the womb around the five-month mark
10) A man spends five months of his life shaving

## Entertainment

1) Nicolas Cage's real name at birth was Nicolas Coppola
2) Oprah's name was a typo; it was supposed to be Orpah
3) Bruce Willis sang a song that went to be No. 5 on the charts
4) Disney doesn't have employees, only cast members
5) Chuck Norris has his own martial arts school called "Chun Kuk Do"

6) The body actor for Darth Vader was banned from the Star Wars conventions for some time because of his constant complaining to George Lucas
7) In 2009, Tina Fey got a record-breaking 22 nominations for an Emmy
8) The creator of the Emmy used his wife as a reference
9) Shirley Dinsdale won the first Emmy in 1949
10) The Best Animated Feature Film category in the Academy Award was only added in 2001

## Astronomy

1) The sun is 4.5 billion years old
2) The proper maps of the moon was made by Galileo
3) Every 27.3 days the moon orbits the earth
4) The color blue in the sky is a mixture of dust and water particles
5) Clouds are made from small drops of water and ice
6) There are million tons of water found in clouds
7) There are 100 different types of clouds

8) You can see 3,000 stars in the night sky with the naked eye
9) The Milky Way has over one billion stars
10) There are stars that are 100 times bigger than the sun

## Moose

1) The moose are powerful swimmers from birth
2) The moose are the largest member of the deer family
3) In Europe, it is called an elk
4) Moose has poor eyesight but has strong sense of smell and hearing
5) Moose weigh 1,000 to 1,800 pounds
6) Moose can live up to 25 years
7) Male moose antlers can reach six feet in length
8) The front legs of a moose are longer than the back legs
9) Female moose never get antlers
10) Moose grow new antlers every year

## Beavers

1) Beavers weigh up to 30 pounds

2) Beavers are 2-3 feet long, not including their tails
3) The teeth of a beaver never stop growing
4) Their front teeth stick out, so they can chew underwater without swallowing water
5) They can remain underwater for 15 minutes before needing air
6) They are monogamous
7) Beavers hate the sound of running water; that's partly why they build dams
8) They can fix a damaged dam in one night
9) The longest beaver dam is 2,750 feet long
10) European and North American beavers will not mate with each other

## Ferrets

1) A female ferret is called a Jill, and a male ferret is called a Hob
2) Ferrets can weigh up to four pounds
3) Ferrets can sleep 18 hours a day
4) Ferrets were first domesticated 2,000 years ago

5) Ferrets cannot survive on their own; generally, they will die within four days if neglected by their pet owners. They are high maintenance pets.
6) A group of ferrets are called a business
7) Queen Victoria raised albino ferrets and would give them as gifts
8) Ferrets are deep sleepers; no amount of poking or prodding will wake them
9) The ferret's name comes from the Latin word "furonem," which means thief
10) After cats and dogs, ferrets are the most popular pet

## Ravens

1) Ravens are the largest bird in the crow family
2) Ravens have a lifespan of 40-70 years
3) Unkindness is the term used to describe a flock of ravens
4) Ravens were considered the bringer of storms and bad weather by the Greeks and Japanese
5) Ravens can imitate other birds within the same vocal range
6) Ravens are considered the most intelligent of birds

7) Ravens get other animals to work for them by making calls to attract them
8) Ravens have been taught to count
9) Ravens are really playful; they were known to wait on the rooftops of supermarkets just to push snow over the head of the consumers!
10) They can live in a variety of places from forests to deserts

## Planets

1) Poor Pluto—it was removed from being called a planet
2) Mercury is one of the hottest planets, but scientists say it may have ice
3) Mars has water, but it's frozen.
4) Venus is the hottest planet
5) Jupiter's gravity is 2½ times greater than Earth's
6) Though it's so large, Jupiter rotates the fastest
7) Uranus is the only planet to rotate on its side
8) Neptune's winds can reach up to 2,100 miles an hour
9) Every 14-15 years, Saturn's rings seem to disappear from Earth's sight
10) Earth's magnetic field protects it from space

# Toothpaste

1) Toothpaste is actually a grinding agent
2) Diacalcium makes up a fifth of what's in toothpaste
3) The flavors of toothpaste are usually plant-based, like spearmint and peppermint
4) Before toothpaste, people used ground eggshells and burnt animal hooves to clean their teeth
5) Colgate marketed the first commercial brand in 1896
6) Twenty-two percent of people leave a glob of toothpaste on the sink
7) Fluoride helps strengthen teeth
8) More people use blue toothbrushes over red ones
9) Someone, among other jobs, squeezes the toothpaste on Prince Charles's toothbrush
10) Over one lifetime, 38.5 days are spent brushing teeth

## Floss

1) Seventy-three percent of Americans rather go grocery shopping than floss
2) North Americans spend two billion dollars a year on tooth cleaning supplies like floss
3) If you don't floss, 35% of your tooth surface is not clean
4) Floss was commercially available in 1882
5) Floss was first made from silk
6) Now floss is made from Gore-tex
7) Around 18 yards of floss are bought by each person each year
8) Dentists think that 122 yards of floss should be bought each year
9) By braiding floss into a rope in 1994, a prison inmate scaled the wall and escaped
10) Worldwide, 28% of people floss, but it's believed that some of them are lying

## Make-Up

1) Make-up first appeared in early Egypt
2) In Biblical times, it was referred to as face painting
3) In the old times ladies put snails on their faces to get rid of wrinkles

4) In Victorian times, only working girls, prostitutes, and the poor wore make-up
5) During the Renaissance, they used arsenic to make their faces pure white
6) Lipstick first become popular because it made women's lips look like the female's lower anatomy
7) The word cosmetics come from the Greek word "kosmos," which means "of this world"
8) Ground fish scales are use as ingredients in some lipsticks and eye shadows
9) Belladonna, a poisonous plant is used to dilate the pupils of women in the 17th to 18th century to look attractive
10) Aztec use red dye that comes from beetles to color their lips and nails red

## Clothes

1) Dry-cleaned clothes last longer
2) Button comes from the French word "bouton," which means knob or bud
3) Buttons were just for decoration when they were first put on clothes

4) Christian Dior in the 1950s designed the pencil skirt and the A-line skirt
5) In the 1500s, designers showed off their work by having dolls wear their fashions
6) In just the last 200 years children started having their own style of clothing
7) The skirt is the second oldest women's garment
8) Anything from 1920-1960 is vintage; the rest is retro
9) In 2300 B.C., a triangular piece of clothing was fashionable for both men and women
10) The bra wasn't patented until 1914

## Water

1) Seventy percent of the earth is covered in water
2) Eighty percent of a baby's weight at birth is water
3) Most fresh water is found under the earth's surface
4) There are 326 million cubic miles of water on earth
5) Flushing the toilet takes up the most of one person's usage of water per day
6) By the time someone is thirsty, they have already lost 1% of the water they need
7) Water can help ease a headache

8) Drinking too much water can lead to a condition known as water intoxication which dilute the sodium level in the blood
9) Drinking adequate amounts of water lessen the risk of an individual to certain types of cancer like colon, bladder and breast cancer
10) One healthy person can drink three gallons of water a day

## Firefighters

1) The English word "firefighter" has been used since 1903
2) In 2008, there were 25 million calls to fire departments in the United States
3) Their jackets can handle temperatures up to 1,200 degrees Fahrenheit
4) Their trucks are usually around 30 feet long
5) Tanker trucks used by firefighters carry 1,000 gallons of water
6) The average ladder used by firefighters can reach up to 40-50 feet in height
7) Seven percent of firefighters worldwide are women
8) The fireman jacket used by firefighters weight 30 pounds

9) Rapid Invitation Team (or R.I.T.) comes in to save trapped firefighters
10) They wear reflective material to see in the dark and fog

## Earth

1) Earth is the fifth largest planet in our solar system
2) Earth is the only planet to have all of these things: solid(ice), liquid(sea) and gas(clouds)
3) Earth is nearly five billion years old
4) Earth is the only planet not to be named after a Greek god
5) The earth travels at 108,000 kilometers per hour
6) The earth is not truly round but more pumpkin-shaped
7) The earth is mostly made of iron, oxygen, and silicone
8) The earth's atmosphere extends out 10,000 kilometers above the surface of the planet
9) The molten core of earth creates a magnetic field
10) It doesn't take 24 hours for the earth to turn completely but 23 hours, 56 minutes, and four seconds

# Wind

1) The wind is powered by the sun
2) Wind currently powers over one million Canadian homes
3) Denmark gets 20% of its energy through wind
4) The windiest place in the world is Port Martin, Antarctica
5) The fastest winds are in a tornado funnel; they reach up to 480 kilometers per hour
6) Wet air is lighter than dry air
7) Warm air rises, even though it's heavier than cool air
8) The strongest wind gust recorded was at a speed of 371 kilometers per hour
9) Wind was used to propel boats in the Nile River in 5000 B.C.
10) In 200 B.C., China used windmills to grind rice and pump water

# Whales

1) The heaviest brain in the world is 20 pounds, and it's a whale's brain
2) The fastest whale can swim 20 miles per hour

3) Killer whales were named as such because they sometimes preyed on large whales and sharks
4) A humpback can eat a ton of food a day
5) A newborn baby blue whale can be 15 feet long
6) Whales are mammals, not fish
7) The blue whale is the largest animal on earth
8) Baleen whales are known to sing
9) Some whales can stay underwater for 90 minutes
10) Whales only sleep with half their brain; that way, they remember to get air and not drown

# Seals

1) There are 33 known species of seals all over the world
2) The popular grey seal goes to Scotland annually to breed
3) They give birth on land, not in water
4) Considering their size, they have more blood than any other animals
5) Some seals can dive 1,000-1,300 feet underwater
6) Seals can stay underwater for up to 30 minutes

7) They're thought to be descendants from bears
8) They detect food with their whiskers
9) A male seal can weigh up to 880 pounds
10) Most seals prefer cold water

# Mountains

1) There are five basic kinds of mountains: Dome, Fold, Fault-block, Volcanic, and Plateau
2) 12% of the world's population make the mountains their homes
3) Since 2003, December 11 is celebrated as International Mountain Day
4) The 50 highest mountains are all in Asia
5) The Alps are the most densely populated mountains
6) The Himalayan Mountains' name means "abode of snow"
7) Mountains take up a fifth of the world's landscape
8) The tallest mountain in the solar system is on Mars
9) The longest mountain range are found under the sea
10) A land mass that rises 1000 feet from the ground is called a mountain

# Medicine

1) Ketchup was sold as medicine in the 1830s
2) In1999, the first fetal surgery was performed
3) The polio vaccine was made in 1952
4) A, B, and O blood types were first discovered in the early 1900s
5) The first heart transplant was done in 1967
6) In 1816, the stethoscope was invented
7) When doctors take the Hippocratic Oath, they swear an oath to the Greek god Apollo
8) In 1884, laughing gas was used as an anesthetic to extract teeth
9) Plastic surgery was first done in 600 B.C.
10) More antibiotics are used on animals than humans

# Foxes

1) Arctic foxes can survive in temperatures of 50 degree Fahrenheit or lower
2) Arctic foxes mate for life
3) Red foxes weigh 20-25 pounds

4) The red fox is the most common specie of fox in the world
5) Arctic foxes live in dens that can be up to 300 years old
6) A fox can hear a watch ticking from 40 yards away
7) Foxes can run up 30 miles per hour
8) Like cats, foxes play with their food before they eat it
9) The scientific name for foxes is Vulpes
10) The male and female fox both take care of their young

## Carrots

1) The largest producer of carrots in the world is China
2) Carrots are called philtron by the ancient Greeks which means "love charm"
3) Ancient Greeks believed that carrots were an aphrodisiac
4) It was once recommended that women eat carrot seeds to stop pregnancy
5) In England, ladies once used carrots as hat decorations
6) China is one of the top producers of carrots in the world today
7) Carrots are the seventh most valuable crop
8) Carrots are 87% water

9) The longest carrot was 17 feet long
10) The heaviest carrot weighed 18.5 pounds

# Bread

1) It takes nine seconds for a combine harvester to get enough wheat for 70 loaves of bread
2) A family of four could have enough bread for 10 years with one acre of wheat
3) The biggest loaf of bread is nine kilometers in length and was baked in Mexico
4) Bread is one food that all races eat
5) In Russia, bread and salt are things of welcoming
6) It is estimated that 12 million loaves are bought in UK every year
7) The breaking of the bread is considered a universal sign of peace
8) Bread is one of the oldest foods in the world
9) Bread was placed in the tombs of the deceased to take to the next life in ancient Egypt
10) It was only in 1928 that pre-sliced breads were made available because they used to believe that pre-sliced bread go stale faster

# Frogs

1) Frogs shed their skin once a week
2) Frogs drink water through their skin and not through their mouths
3) A group of frogs is called an army
4) Not all frogs croak; some whistle and even chirp
5) The eggs of tree frogs fall from the trees where they were laid to their watery homes below
6) Tree frogs change color according to the temperatures
7) Tree frogs were one of the few survivors of the Mount St. Helens blast because they bury themselves in the dirt.
8) In Egypt, frog symbolizes life and fertility
9) The size of the smallest frog in the world is just about less of an inch long
10) The goliath frog is the largest frog in the world

# Jewelry

1) One hundred percent gold is too soft to make into jewelry
2) It is believed that genital piercings can improve one's love life

3) Men first wore jewelry as amulets in war
4) The largest diamond in the world was called the Cullinan
5) The largest diamond weighs 1 1/3 pounds
6) More than half (58.3%) of gold in the market is 14k
7) The value of emeralds, rubies, and sapphires depends on their color
8) A natural pearl feels like grit on teeth
9) The tradition of giving diamond ring for engagement started in 1477 when Maximillian of Austria gave a diamond ring to his fiancée Mary of Burgundy

## Allergies

1) Asthma is a type of allergy
2) 5.5% of North Americans die due to insect stings
3) One hundred fifty people die from allergic reactions each year
4) Pemphigoid Genstitionis is when a pregnant woman is allergic to the baby inside her womb
5) Aquagenic Urticaria is an allergy to water

6) It's estimated that five million children suffer from food allergies in North America
7) In America one of five individuals suffer from allergies
8) 17 million outpatient visits in America is due to allergies
9) In the U.S. allergies rank 5th in the leading chronic diseases
10) The percentage of people who suffers from peanut allergies in the US in the past 10 years has doubled

## Guinea Pigs

1) Guinea pigs on average live for 4-5 years
2) There are nine different species of guinea pigs
3) Eight million years ago, guinea pigs were over nine feet long and weighed 1,500 pounds
4) The word pig, in the name guinea pig, does not indicate any relation between pigs and guinea pigs
5) They are also called cavies or cavy
6) Guinea pigs are rodents but are not nocturnal like most

7) At three hours old, the baby guinea pig can run
8) A baby guinea pig is called a pup
9) Guinea pigs are herbivores
10) When guinea pigs are happy, they bounce around; this is called "popcorning"

## Sticky Notes

1) Dr. Spenser Silver developed a repositionable glue but don't have an idea on what to use it for.
2) It was Arthur Fry that had the idea to use the adhesive of Dr. Silver to put paper in place
3) Post it notes were introduced in the U.S. in the 1980s
4) It takes 506,880,000 sticky notes to circle the world
5) In 1989, a sticky note left on a door when a hurricane hit was found to be still on the door after three days.
6) It survived a 500 miles per hour flight from Las Vegas to Minneapolis on the nose of the plane
7) In 2000, they made a line of dresses which used sticky notes
8) In 2009, they made a sticky note that was 30% recycled paper

9) Post it is yellow in color because they used yellow paper initially in the development stage of the product
10) There are over 600 products that are based on the sticky notes concept

## Zebras

1) There are three different breeds of zebras
2) Zebras are also called ungulates, which means hoofed animals
3) Baby zebras can run an hour after they're born
4) They can run as fast as 40 miles per hour
5) Ancient Rome called Zebra "hippotigris"
6) No zebra has the same stripe patterns
7) They can weigh around 500-600 pounds
8) They have long jaws so they can eat a mouthful with their eyes up and at the sides to watch for their predators.
9) Twenty-eight years is a zebra's average lifespan
10) A group of zebras is called a dazzle

## Skunks

1) Skunks belong to the weasel family

2) A skunk can spray someone from 10 feet away
3) Skunks aim for the eyes to blind their enemies
4) Skunks can and will eat a rattlesnake
5) Foxes and raccoons will share a burrow with a skunk
6) Skunks are very social animals
7) Skunks litters have 2-6 kits (babies) in them
8) Skunks are also called polecats
9) There are 10 different types of skunks
10) A group of skunks are called a surfeit

## Bees

1) Bees have been around for over 30 million years
2) A bee is the only bug that makes something that we eat
3) A honeybee's wings go up and down 11,400 times a minute
4) A bee will visit 50-100 flowers per trip
5) Bees communicate with each other by dancing
6) Bees must eat 17-20 pounds of honey to produce one pound of bees wax
7) When stressed, bees will eat one of their own

8) They must be taught to make honey; they don't know it by instinct
9) A queen bee can lay 200,000 eggs a year
10) Honeybees have five eyes, two at the sides of their heads and three at the center

## Laundry

1) Liquid Tide glows under black light
2) Native Americans used soap nuts to clean their clothes
3) Tide first made detergent in the 1930s
4) Tide was the first company to create detergent that didn't leave clothes stiff
5) Salt can be used to clean hard stains in clothes
6) It was in the 1930s that the electrical washing machines were invented
7) On an average 8 to 10 loads of laundry per week are done by an American family
8) Davidson University in North Carolina gives free laundry service to its students
9) Laundry cast members in Walt Disney do an average of 285,000 pounds of laundry each day

10) The fragrance found in detergents are made from phthalates – a

# Squirrels

1) Squirrels can be found in almost all parts of the world from arid deserts to tropical forests and frozen tundra
2) Beside nuts, they love eating insects
3) Their name comes from the Greek world "skiouros," which means "shadow tail"
4) There are over 200 types of squirrels
5) Flying squirrels can glide over 150 feet
6) The smallest squirrel is four inches long
7) The largest one is 2 feet, 5 inches long
8) Squirrels have a 2 to 5 years lifespan
9) For the Native American, squirrels symbolize trust, preparation and thriftiness
10) There are many types of squirrels about 265 squirrels worldwide

# Dance

1) Male dancers lift 1½ tons of ballerinas in one performance

2) Most ballerinas wear out 2-3 shoes a week
3) A tutu can cost up to $2,000 to make
4) One tutu takes 60-90 hours to make
5) Social dancing (club dancing or with friends) burns the same amount of calories as a four-mile walk
6) Tango started in the city slums of Buenos Aires
7) The Cha-cha was created in Cuba
8) Foxtrot was created by actor Harry Fox
9) The German word "waltzen," meaning to turn, is where the Waltz got its name
10) Tap dancing was popular among Africans in the early 1900s

## Singing

1) Singing releases a hormone that makes humans happy
2) Anyone can learn to sing well with proper training
3) Singing 10 minutes a day can improve a person's singing voice
4) Singing relieves stress and tension
5) One's personality can be figured out through their music choices
6) Classical music is good for relaxing
7) It has been proven to lower blood pressure

8) If the right pitch is reached, you can shatter a wine glass
9) The middle C is the top of a singing range for a male and the lowest for a female
10) Dogs and cats can also sing, not just birds

## Alligators

1) Male alligators can reach up to 1,000 pounds
2) Airplanes were known to hit not only birds but also alligators
3) Alligators can only run at their top speed for a few feet
4) Their name comes from a Spanish word that means "the lizard"
5) The largest one measured at 19 feet, 2 inches
6) Alligators on average live to be 50 years old
7) Only two countries have alligators, the U.S. and China
8) Alligators swallow their food whole
9) Alligators won't mate until they reach six feet in length
10) They lay 40-45 eggs

# Sharks

1) There are 350 types of sharks
2) The smallest shark is the size of a human hand
3) If given a good meal, they can go for three months without eating
4) Sharks don't sleep
5) Sharks can't get cancer
6) They were around before dinosaurs
7) Sharks bodies are so heavy that if they stop moving, they sink
8) More people are killed by bees than sharks
9) Ninety percent of people attacked by sharks live
10) Sharks attack more males than females

# Venus flytrap

1) Venus flytraps are closely related to sundews
2) It takes 10 days for the Venus flytrap to digest its prey
3) Venus flytraps are native to North Carolina and South Carolina
4) They are illegal to dig out of their natural environment

5) *Dionaeamuscipula* is its technical name
6) It lure in prey with the smell it emits
7) Venus flytraps can survive without food for 1 to 2 months
8) It has a lifespan of 25 years
9) It needs 14 hours of sunlight everyday to live
10) It needs to be watered with distilled water or rain water because the chemicals in tap water will kill it

# Prisons

1) Fifty percent of homeless-looking people get longer jail time than good-looking people
2) Two hundred new jails are made each day in the U.S.
3) Worldwide, more men are raped in prisons each year than women outside
4) The world's smallest jail is 270 square feet
5) 182 people died in jail in 2005 and 2006 in the United States
6) Worldwide, over 75% of women in prison are single mothers
7) Twenty-two percent of Australians have an ancestor who's a convict
8) Alcatraz is the most popular (well-known) prison to date

9) In the prohibition era, some towns sold their jails
10) In the US 4 out of 10 prisoners will return to jail after three years of being released

## Cartoons

1) Oswald, the lucky rabbit, was one of Disney's first characters
2) Speedy Mouse's cousin's name is Slowpoke
3) Sylvester the Cat, won an Academy Award for Cartoon Short Subject category
4) Wile E. Coyote scenes were edited in the 1980s for being too violent
5) The name of Pepe Le Pew's love interest is Penelope Pussycat
6) Tweety Bird was supposed to be called Orson
7) Mel Blanc did Daffy Duck's voice for 52 years
8) Droll is what a boring cartoon is called
9) Donald Duck's middle name is Fauntleroy
10) Mickey Mouse was supposed to be called Mortimer, but Walt Disney's wife found it creepy

# Insects

1) The male cicada can be heard 440 yards away
2) The longest bug is a walking stick at 1.3 feet
3) The male ladybug is smaller than the female
4) Ladybugs are technically beetles
5) There are 300,000 types of beetles in the world
6) A honeybee can lift 300 times its own weight
7) The average mosquito has 47 teeth
8) Grasshoppers can draw blood when they kick
9) A cockroach can live nine days without its head
10) Wasps kill more people than snakes

# Fabric

1) Flax is the earliest known textile
2) Cotton and wool were already used as natural fabric in 3000 B.C.
3) Silk was made into fabric in China in 2500 B.C.

4) China has been the largest maker of silk for the past 100 years
5) Microfiber was invented 20 years ago in Japan
6) Acrylic is a man-made fabric designed to make other fabrics stronger
7) Nylon is also man-made and took the place of silk in stockings
8) The best cotton still comes from Egypt
9) Bamboo is a grass that can be made into fabric
10) The first man-made fabric came in 1910

## Snakes

1) There are more than 3000 types of snakes that exists
2) An anaconda can be as big as 38 feet long
3) They use their fork tongues to smell things
4) Poisonous snakes have larger heads because that's where they store their venom
5) Snakes have more than 230 teeth
6) Snakes mate in cooler climates
7) Snakes are considered the deadliest animal in the world because snakes kill 100,000 individuals each year
8) 350 types of snakes have venom that are deadly to humans

9) Some places in China considered snakes inside the house as good omen
10) The smallest snake is about the size of a toothpick and is about 4 inches in length and is called the thread snake

# Cakes

1) In the Celtic tradition, it was believed that a cake rolled down a hill and didn't break is a sign of good fortune
2) Cheesecake is believed to have been served at the first Olympic Games
3) Red velvet cake gets its red color from the red dye that comes from crushed beetles
4) People once put coins and rings in cakes. The ones who found them were to marry the one they loved or were to find love soon
5) In 17th century England an unmarried individual would put fruitcake under their pillow to dream about their future love
6) The word "cake" came from the Norse word "kaka"
7) During ancient times, a loaf of bread is broken on top of the head of the bride or pieces of bread are thrown at her
8) The Chinese would bake moon cakes during Harvest Moon Festival to honor their moon goddess

9) Russians baked sun cakes which are thin pancakes in honor of their deity Maslenitsa
10) Cheesecakes are not really cakes but are actually custard pies

# Fur

1) Fake fur was first made in 1929
2) Fake fur was first commercially available in the 1950s
3) Fake fur is not warm and insulating like real fur
4) It takes 500-1000 years for fake fur to break down
5) It takes 60% less energy to make a fake fur coat than a real one
6) Fake fur helps stop the killing of millions of animals for their fur
7) Fake fur is easily manipulated more than real fur, which made them versatile to many styles
8) Real fur went down in sales in the 1980s by 50%
9) Wigs have been made from faux fur
10) Real fur is water resistant

# Snow Globes

1) Snow globes were created in France in the early 1800s
2) In the 1920s, most snow globes were made in Germany
3) The first snow globe was palm-sized and had the Eiffel Tower in it
4) In the 1950s, snow globes became oversold and considered tacky
5) In the 1970s, they started designer snow globes; they were more elaborate
6) The most famous snow globe was featured in the movie *Citizen Kane*
7) Erwin Perzy first patented the snow globe
8) In 2005, inflatable snow globes started to be sold
9) Snow globes became popular at Halloween for their designs of soaring bats and ghosts
10) Snow globes were used mostly to represent innocent times

## Art

1) Picasso started the cubism movement
2) It took Leonardo da Vinci 12 years to paint the lips of Mona Lisa
3) Most artists are left-handed

4) Red Vineyard at Arles was the only painting Van Gogh sold during his lifetime
5) Leonardo da Vinci was a vegetarian and would buy caged animals and would set them free
6) "The Pieta" was the only work Michaelangelo signed with his name
7) Pablo Picasso was a suspect in the theft of the Mona Lisa in 1911 but was later cleared and released
8) English artist Andy Brown created the portrait of Queen Elizabeth using 1000 pieces of teabags
9) It was said that Picasso learned to draw first before he started walking
10) French painter, Paul Gaugin was one of the laborers of the Panama canal

## Groundhogs

1) Groundhogs are also called whistle pigs and woodchucks
2) Groundhogs can grow to be two feet in length and no bigger
3) Two to three years is the average lifespan of a groundhog
4) Groundhogs are related to squirrels
5) Groundhogs can swim and climb trees

6) Forty feet long and five feet deep is the size of a groundhog burrow
7) The male groundhog leaves the den before the babies are born
8) A groundhog's accuracy on Groundhog Day is 37% for predicting spring
9) A groundhog takes one breath every six minutes when hibernating
10) A young groundhog is called a kit

# Bubbles

1) Bubbles can be in a wide range of colors
2) The biggest bubble formed was 105.4 cubic feet
3) The wetter the bubble wand, the easier it is to make bubbles
4) Windy days are bad for bubble blowing, as the bubble will not form
5) In 1999, 23,680 people got together in London to blow bubbles
6) A bubble wall was made in 1997 that was 156 feet wide and 13 feet tall
7) In 2001, the record for the most bubbles inside one another was 12
8) The longest bubble was 105 feet long
9) Children have been blowing bubbles for 400 years
10) A bubble will not form inside a vacuum because of the lack of exterior air

pressure to counteract the pressure from the inside

## Candles

1) Candles are used in seven out of 10 households
2) The average candle user burns candles three times a week
3) The most important factor of a candle is its scent
4) Candles continue to grow in sales no matter the economy
5) The typical candle burns for three hours
6) Forty-two percent of candles are burned in the living room
7) Candle sales are about $2 billion each year
8) There are over 350 candle-making companies in the U.S. alone
9) Worldwide, 96% of candles are bought by women
10) Seventy-six percent of candles bought are for the holidays worldwide

## Salamanders

1) Salamander means "fire lover" or "fire lizard"
2) They can live for about 30 years
3) They have 10 times the amount of DNA in one cell than a human
4) Tiger salamanders don't drink
5) There are 500 different kinds of salamanders
6) Giant salamanders can weigh 140 pounds
7) Newt is a term used for a salamander that spends most of his time on land
8) Some salamanders can shed their tails when attacked
9) Tiger salamanders have no voice
10) They are nocturnal

Made in the USA
Monee, IL
10 April 2021